FIRST PRESBYTERIAN
CHURCH
ROYAL OAK

In memory of
Eleanor Lawle

Given By
Janet Meissner

1986

CONSIDER
THE LILIES

CONSIDER THE LILIES

Plants of the Bible

John & Katherine Paterson

PAINTINGS BY

Anne Ophelia Dowden

THOMAS Y. CROWELL   NEW YORK

Consider the Lilies: Plants of the Bible
Text copyright © 1986 by John and Katherine Paterson
Illustrations copyright © 1986 by Anne Ophelia Dowden
Printed in the U.S.A. All rights reserved.
Designed by Harriett Barton
1   2   3   4   5   6   7   8   9   10
First Edition

Library of Congress Cataloging in Publication Data
Paterson, John (John Barstow)
    Consider the lilies.

    Summary: Presents botanical illustrations of familiar
and exotic flowers, trees, and plants mentioned in the
accompanying Bible verses and selections.
    1. Plants in the Bible—Juvenile literature.
[1. Plants in the Bible]   I. Paterson, Katherine.
II. Dowden, Anne Ophelia Todd, 1907–   ill.
III. Title.
BS665.P37 1986   220.8′581   85-43603
ISBN 0-690-04461-5
ISBN 0-690-04463-1 (lib. bdg.)

For Lauren Wohl

from

John & Katherine Paterson

&

Anne Ophelia Dowden

ACKNOWLEDGMENTS

The artist wishes to thank all the many people who provided both invaluable information and plant specimens to paint. She is particularly indebted to the following: at the Brooklyn Botanic Garden, Dr. Thomas Delendick, Dr. Stephen K-M Tim, Mrs. Nancy Tim, Miss Marie Giasi; at the New York Botanical Garden, Dr. Rupert Barneby; at Neot Kedumim (The Gardens of Israel), Mr. Nogah Hareuveni, Mr. Paul Steinfeld; in Jerusalem, Israel, Mrs. Nellie Stavisky; at the En Gedi Field School, Israel, Mr. Zvika Livneh; at the U. S. Department of Agriculture Research Center, Dr. Charles R. Gunn; at the Bailey Hortorium of Cornell University, Dr. William J. Dress; at Pennsylvania State University, Dr. Charles W. Mann, Dr. Guy M. McKee; at Adolph Coors Company, Golden, Colorado, Mr. David A. Thomas; in Fishertown, Pennsylvania, Mr. and Mrs. Obie Snider, Mr. and Mrs. Frank Gajer; in Norfolk, Connecticut, Dr. and Mrs. Richard Barstow.

For the plant identifications used in this book, the chief authority is Professor Michael Zohary, Hebrew University of Jerusalem.

All plants pictured in this book are exactly ⅔ natural size.

Anemone

"Consider how the lilies grow in the fields; they do not work, they do not spin; and yet, I tell you, even Solomon in all his splendor was not attired like one of these. But if that is how God clothes the grass in the fields, which is there today, and tomorrow is thrown on the stove, will he not all the more clothe you? How little faith you have! No, do not ask anxiously, 'What are we to eat? What are we to drink? What shall we wear?' All these are things for the heathen to run after, not for you, because your heavenly Father knows you need them all. Set your mind on God's kingdom and his justice before anything else, and all the rest will come to you as well. . . ."

Matthew 6:28B–33
New English Bible

Contents

Laurel

Introduction

A dove bearing a sprig of olive in her beak, a vine loaded with sweet purple grapes, a wise man presenting a cask of fragrant myrrh—even though we are separated from the world of the Bible by many years and even more miles, these familiar pictures from those times and that place speak immediately to our imaginations. Doesn't it follow, then, that the more we know about the world of the Bible, the more its words and images will have meaning for us? The purpose of this book is to take a close look at some of the plants mentioned in the Bible. The plants are not themselves the center of the passages in which they occur. The sprig of olive, the grapevine, the myrrh—all point beyond themselves to a deeper meaning.

This book has been divided into three sections: Revelation, Necessity, and Celebration. You will soon see, however, that a plant could belong in more than one section. The grapevine, for example, while it was certainly necessary for life, was also, in a very real sense, a revelation of God's care for his people, and its wine was a symbol of celebration.

Over the centuries a great deal of research has been done to identify the plants of the Bible. While everyone agrees that figs and dates and lentils and barley are the plants we know today by the same names, no one is sure exactly what plants are meant by certain other references, such as gall and balm and weeds. In part, this confusion arose because the people who translated the ancient Hebrew or Greek texts did not know the botany of the Holy Land. They often used names like "lily," "rose," and "willow" for plants that certainly were not lilies or roses or willows. Modern scholars who have studied both the ancient words and the plants of Palestine have solved some of the questions, but there is still uncertainty and disagreement about many Bible plants.

In this book, as in the Bible, there is an account of a garden planted before history and a city established after history has come to its close. In the midst of both grows the same tree, the tree of life. Now, the tree of life is not one that will be found in any book of botany. But the Biblical writers chose to use the image of a tree because a tree is something all of their readers would be familiar with. Some readers might imagine one kind of tree, and some another, but everyone can see a tree in his mind's eye.

People can best visualize unimaginable things by means of things they know. The writers of the Bible understood this. That is why in telling us stories about God's mysterious dealings with the world, they have used what we can see and touch and smell and hear and taste to point us to truths beyond our experience.

With pictures and text, this book considers trees and flowers and plants that appear in the Bible story. Perhaps, through these, we may catch a glimpse of the tree of life that grows in our deepest hearts.

Olive

REVELATION

At the end of forty days Noah sent forth a dove, to see if
    the waters had subsided from the face of the ground;
but the dove found no place to set her foot, and she returned
    to him to the ark, for the waters were still on the face
    of the whole earth.
So Noah put forth his hand and took her and brought her
    into the ark.
He waited another seven days, and again he sent forth the dove
    out of the ark;
and the dove came back to him in the evening, and lo, in her
    mouth a freshly plucked olive leaf;
so Noah knew that the waters had subsided from the earth.

after Genesis 8:8–11

The Tree of the Knowledge of Good and Evil

The Book of Genesis tells how God created the world and all plant and animal life, and, finally, a man and a woman, made in the image of God. The following story tells what happened when the man and woman disobeyed God and ate the fruit of the tree of the knowlege of good and evil.

When the Lord God created the world, he planted in the east a garden called Eden, which means "delight." And it was a place of delight for the man and woman whom he had made. However, in that garden grew two trees, unlike the others. One was called the tree of life, and the other the tree of the knowledge of good and evil. "You may eat of any of the trees of the garden," God told them, "except the tree of the knowledge of good and evil. If you eat the fruit of that tree, you will surely die."

At that time the man and woman did not know death or even that they were naked, because fear and shame had not yet entered the world.

But one day the serpent, who of all God's creatures was the most cunning, put a question to the woman. "Is it true that God has forbidden you to eat any fruit of the trees of the garden?"

"No," she said. "We may eat from all of the trees of the garden except for one. God said we must not eat the fruit of that tree, or even touch it, for if we do, we will die."

"You wouldn't die," the serpent said. "God doesn't want you to eat that fruit because he knows that if you do, your eyes will be opened and you will be like gods, knowing both good and evil."

Now suddenly the fruit of that tree looked especially beautiful and delicious to the woman, and she longed for the knowledge that it would give her. So she took some of the fruit and ate it and gave some to her husband and he ate as well. Their eyes were opened, and for the first time the man and the woman knew that they were naked. They were ashamed and tried to make themselves coverings sewn from fig leaves.

In the cool of the afternoon, God came for a visit, but he could not find the man and the woman. "Where are you?" God called.

The man answered, "I heard the sound of you walking in the garden and I was afraid because I was naked, so I hid myself."

"Who told you that you were naked?" God asked. "Did you eat fruit from the tree that I forbade?"

"It was the woman," said the man, "the one you made and gave to me to be my companion. It was she who gave me the fruit."

Then the Lord turned to the woman. "What have you done?"

The woman answered, "It was the serpent. He tricked me."

God took the skins of animals and made clothing for the man and the woman, and he drove them out of the delightful garden and into the world, where they would know pain and grief and death. And God set an angel with a fiery sword to guard the entrance of Eden, lest the man and woman try to return and take and eat the fruit from the tree of life and live forever in the state of shame and misery to which they had fallen.

after Genesis 3

Crab apple

Apple *Malus* sp.

The tree of the knowledge of good and evil, like the tree of life, is not a plant that grows in nature. It is a mythical tree, and the Bible gives it no name at all. In spite of this, the Western world has for centuries visualized the forbidden fruit as an apple. Perhaps we owe this image to the many medieval European paintings of the Temptation of Adam and Eve, in which the artists, rather than depicting a mythical fruit, placed an apple in Eve's hand.

There are, however, several definite references to apples in the Bible, and they have caused great controversy. Scholars disagree as to whether the old Hebrew word tappuah *properly refers to the apple or to some other fruit—perhaps the apricot. It is not certain that apples grew in Biblical Palestine, though we know that they were cultivated by the Egyptians, and that the Romans at the time of Christ had more than twenty varieties. None of these ancient apples resembled the large, beautiful fruits we know today; they were probably more like the modern crab apple pictured here.*

Whatever the fruit might have been, it inspired a number of Biblical authors. "A word fitly spoken," says the writer of Proverbs, "is like apples of gold in settings of silver." "Comfort me with apples," says the writer of the Song of Songs, "for I am sick with love."

19

Balm of Gilead

Jeremiah, whose name means "God hurled," was born in a tiny village northeast of Jerusalem, and before long, perhaps while he was still in his teens, he had been hurled into the midst of his nation's most terrifying crisis. He was a prophet, faithful to God but unpopular among the people, for the young Jeremiah had declared that the Babylonians would destroy the nation, because the children of Israel had forgotten their God.

Jeremiah took his sermon about God's judgment to the gate of the temple in Jerusalem. He called on all who entered to change their lives, for, as he told them, God despises religious ceremony unless it is accompanied by righteous living. The priests thought Jeremiah was irreligious and the rulers thought he was unpatriotic. Others thought he was crazy. He was laughed at, flogged, put in stocks, and jailed, but he could not be silenced. Even from prison he dictated his sermons to his friend Baruch, who took them out and read them aloud.

The worst suffering for Jeremiah was not the flogging or the imprisonment, but the painful message he felt compelled to preach. He loved his nation. It grieved him to think that she must suffer.

> *"For the wound of the daughter of my people is*
> *my heart wounded,*
> *I mourn, and dismay has taken hold on me.*
> *Is there no balm in Gilead?*
> *Is there no physician there?"*

The Babylonians came. They laid waste to the countryside and were on the verge of capturing Jerusalem just as Jeremiah had foretold. Yet, on the eve of destruction, Jeremiah did a strange thing. He bought a piece of real estate, a field near his home village. He paid seventeen shekels of silver for it, had the deed signed, sealed, and witnessed, and then instructed Baruch to put the deed in an earthenware jar, so that it could be preserved for a long time. For just as he believed that God would surely destroy the nation of Judah, Jeremiah believed that God would build it up again. "Is there no balm in Gilead?" Jeremiah cried out and answered his own question by refusing to despair. God would not forsake his people, no matter how faithless they had been.

As the spiritual attests:

> *"There is a balm in Gilead to make the wounded whole;*
> *There is a balm in Gilead to heal the sinsick soul."*

21

Balm of Gilead *Commiphora opobalsamum*
Sweet gum *Liquidambar orientalis*

Balm of Gilead refers to a fragrant resin that is obtained from cuts in the bark of trees and is used for both perfumes and medicines. Several quite different plants produce such resins, and no one is sure which one Jeremiah means in this passage.

One kind of balm, from Commiphora, *has for centuries been called Balm of Gilead by European herbalists and doctors, and under that name it was in all pharmacopoeias until very recent times. Its fragrant resin oozes from the branches in green droplets that accumulate in clumps. As they solidify, they turn brown and then drop to the ground. This substance was a valuable commodity, imported by Arab spice traders long before it was recorded in the Bible, and it is the "balm" or "spice" in many Bible references.*

But the Balm of Gilead of Jeremiah may have come from a different tree. This might have been the Jericho balsam, but a more likely possibility is Liquidambar, *which produces the gum known as storax or stacte, still used in medicine. It is a close and almost identical relative of the tree Americans call red gum or sweet gum.*

22

Commiphora

Liquidambar

The Wormwood and the Gall

There is a tradition that Jeremiah is the author of the Book of Lamentations. Probably he is not, but certainly whoever wrote it was his spiritual child.

"I am the man who has seen affliction under [God's] wrath;
he has driven and brought me into darkness without
     any light;
surely against me he turns his hand again and again the
     whole day long. . . .
He drove into my heart the arrows of his quiver;
I have become the laughingstock of all peoples, the burden
     of their songs all day long.
He has filled me with bitterness, he has sated me with
     wormwood.

He has made my teeth grind on gravel, and made me cower
    in ashes;
my soul is bereft of peace, I have forgotten what happiness
    is;
so I say, 'Gone is my glory, my expectation from the Lord.'
Remember my affliction and my bitterness, the wormwood
    and the gall!
My soul continually thinks of it and is bowed down
    within me.
But this I call to mind, and therefore I have hope:
The steadfast love of the Lord never ceases, his mercies
    never come to an end;
they are new every morning; great is thy faithfulness.
'The Lord is my portion,' says my soul, 'therefore I will
    hope in him.'

Lamentations 3:1–3, 13–24
Revised Standard Version

Wormwood

Poison hemlock

White wormwood   *Artemisia herba-alba*
Poison hemlock   *Conium maculatum*

Wormwood is a name given to several different artemisias—plants related to mugwort and to our Western sagebrush. The passage may refer to the species pictured here, which is very common in the Holy Land. These plants all have a bitter taste and a strong odor, and most have foliage made silvery by a dense coat of minute hairs. The bitter taste and strong smell of wormwood account for both its symbolic and practical uses. The Hebrews thought of bitter things as poisonous and thus as symbols of calamity and sorrow, but they used wormwood as a seasoning, a tonic, and a worm medicine.

Gall is mentioned several times in the Bible. It refers to the juice of a poisonous and bitter plant, but there is no way of knowing exactly which plant. It might be the colocynth, a kind of gourd with a bitter, medicinally useful pulp, or possibly the thorn apple, which Americans call jimson weed. But probably the best guess is the poison hemlock, the plant that poisoned Socrates and served in medicine as a sedative and antispasmodic. It was also considered to be a plant of ill omen, associated with witches and evil spirits.

27

New Life Out of Parched Ground

When the Babylonians captured Jerusalem, they drove many from the city. Out of the despair of the Babylonian Exile rose the voice of a prophet-poet whose words are found in the second part of the book of Isaiah. Like Jeremiah, he believed God would forgive the exiles and restore Israel to them. And he gave them new ideas about what it meant to be chosen by God. To be chosen meant to be chosen to serve, to become one who suffered for others and whose task was to bring all nations to know the graciousness of God.

When the poor and needy seek water, and there is none,
    and their tongue is parched with thirst,
I the Lord will answer them, I the God of Israel will not
    forsake them.
I will open rivers on the bare heights, and fountains
    in the midst of the valleys;
I will make the wilderness a pool of water, and the dry land
    springs of water.
I will put in the wilderness the cedar, the acacia, the
    myrtle, and the olive;
I will set in the desert the cypress, the plane and the pine
    together;

that men may see and know, may consider and understand
   together,
that the hand of the Lord has done this. . . .

[The Servant of the Lord] grew up before him like a young
   plant, and like a root out of dry ground;
he had no form or comeliness that we should look at him,
   and no beauty that we should desire him.
He was despised and rejected by men; a man of sorrows,
   and acquainted with grief,
and as one from whom men hide their faces he was despised,
   and we esteemed him not.
Surely he has borne our griefs and carried our sorrows; yet
   we esteemed him stricken, smitten by God, and afflicted.
But he was wounded for our transgressions, he was bruised
   for our iniquities:
upon him was the chastisement that made us whole, and with
   his stripes we are healed. . . .

It is too light a thing that you should be my servant to
   raise up the tribes of Jacob and to restore the
   preserved of Israel;
I will give you as a light to the nations, that my salvation
   may reach to the end of the earth.

Isaiah 41:17–20; 53:2–5; 49:6

Revised Standard Version

Cedar of Lebanon *Cedrus libani*

Cypress *Cupressus sempervirens*

Acacia *Acacia raddiana*

Oleaster *Elaeagnus angustifolia*

The ancient Hebrew names of the trees mentioned in this passage have been translated in many different ways. The "plane tree," for example, has been called "fir tree" and is possibly the tree now known as Aleppo pine, while the "pine" may be the Brutian pine. There is no question about the cedar, often called the "Prince of Trees." In the time of Solomon, majestic cedars grew in abundance on the mountains of Lebanon and were brought to Jerusalem for the construction of the temple. The cypress of Palestine, a shorter, broader variety of the tall pointed tree so common in Italian gardens, was sometimes called "gopher wood" and was the material used in Noah's ark.

Acacia, the "shittim wood" referred to often in the Bible, has many uses. Fine-grained and durable, its wood was suitable for beautiful things like the Ark of the Covenant, the altar of the tabernacle, and the mummy coffins of the Egyptians. Various species of acacia also provide perfumes, gum arabic, medicine, food for cattle, and firewood. The "olive tree" of this passage is sometimes translated "oil tree" and may be the oleaster rather than the cultivated olive. Its fruits, which yield a rather inferior oil, can be pounded and made into a kind of bread. Myrtle is a fragrant-leafed evergreen used with palm and willow branches in the Festival of the Booths.

30

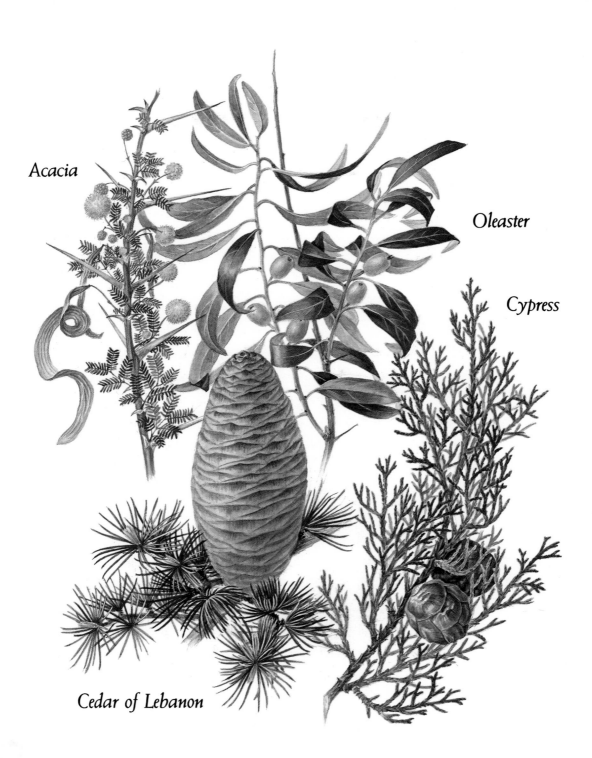

Acacia

Oleaster

Cypress

Cedar of Lebanon

Wheat and Weeds and a Mustard Seed

When Jesus announced the good news of the Kingdom of God to his neighbors and kinsfolk in Nazareth, he read from the words of the prophet-poet of the exile:

"The spirit of the Lord is upon me because he has anointed me to preach good news to the poor; he has sent me to heal the brokenhearted, to preach freedom for those who are captives and the recovering of sight to the blind, to let the bruised go free, and proclaim the year of the Lord's favor." (*after* Isaiah 61:1–2)

He preached about the coming of the Kingdom of Heaven, but he demonstrated the meaning of this phrase in very down-to-earth language and action. He healed the sick, fed the hungry, had dinner with outcasts, and allowed prostitutes to wash his feet.

Do you wonder about the Kingdom of Heaven? Jesus asked his followers. It is like this: A man planted a field of wheat, but his enemy came in the night and sowed weed seeds among the wheat. Now the weed known as darnel looks very much like wheat as it grows, but when the heads of the wheat began to fill out, the man's servants could tell there was darnel growing in the field. The servants were surprised, because they knew they had planted only good seed in the field; but the master realized that an enemy had sown the darnel. He told the servants to let it grow up along with the wheat because he did not want to risk pulling up good wheat along with the weed. "At harvest time I will tell the reapers, 'Gather the darnel first, and tie it into bundles for burning; then collect the wheat into my barn.' "

Or, Jesus said, the Kingdom of Heaven is like a mustard seed which when the farmer planted it, was the smallest of all his seeds, but it grew up larger than any plant in his garden. It was more like a tree, large enough for birds to come and roost among its branches.

In this way Jesus taught that the kingdom, which seemed so tiny and weak, so easily invaded by evil, would grow and flourish.

after Matthew 13:24–32

Mustard

Darnel

Wheat

Wheat *Triticum aestivum*
Darnel *Lolium temulentum*
Mustard *Brassica nigra*

For more than 8,000 years, various species of wheat have been cultivated in Asia Minor, and in Bible times, wheat was the main field crop. Since it was grown without irrigation, it suffered seriously in years of drought, and disastrous famines often resulted.

The "weeds" referred to here were probably darnel grass or "tares," a hardy grass that grows only in grain fields. Before its seed heads form, it looks very much like wheat, and its seeds are about the same size and shape as wheat seeds, so they easily become mixed with the threshed grain. They not only adulterate the wheat but also can carry a poisonous fungus that causes blindness or even death.

The mustard seed in this passage is probably that of the common black mustard. In powdered form, these seeds have since earliest times been used for flavoring and medicine, but the Hebrews valued them chiefly for the oil they produce. In northern gardens, mustard is usually no more than three or four feet tall, but in hot countries it sometimes grows ten to fifteen feet high, with a stalk as thick as a man's arm.

Fruit of the Vine

Jesus said to his disciples:

"I am the true vine, and my Father is the vinedresser. Every branch of mine that bears no fruit, he takes away, and every branch that does bear fruit he prunes, that it may bear more fruit. You are already made clean by the word which I have spoken to you. Abide in me and I in you. As the branch cannot bear fruit by itself, unless it abides in the vine, neither can you, unless you abide in me.

"I am the vine, you are the branches. He who abides in me, and I in him, he it is that bears much fruit, for apart from me you can do nothing. If a man does not abide in me, he is cast forth as a branch and withers; and the branches are gathered, thrown into the fire and burned. If you abide in me, and my words abide in you, ask whatever you will, and it shall be done for you. By this my father is glorified, that you bear much fruit, and so prove to be my disciples.

"You did not choose me, but I chose you and appointed you that you should go and bear fruit and that your fruit should abide."

John 15: 1–8, 16
Revised Standard Version

Let me sing for my beloved a love song concerning his vineyard:
My beloved had a vineyard on a very fertile hill.
He digged it and cleared it of stones,
    and planted it with choice vines;
he built a watchtower in the midst of it,
    and hewed out a wine vat in it;
and he looked for it to yield grapes,
    but it yielded wild grapes.

And now, O inhabitants of Jerusalem and men of Judah,
    judge, I pray you, between me and my vineyard.
What more was there to do for my vineyard,
    that I have not done in it?
When I looked for it to yield grapes,
    why did it yield wild grapes?

Isaiah 5: 1–4
Revised Standard Version

Beware of false prophets, who come to you in sheep's clothing but inwardly are ravenous wolves. You will know them by their fruits. Are grapes gathered from thorns, or figs from thistles? So, every sound tree bears good fruit, but the bad tree bears evil fruit. . . . Thus you will know them by their fruits.

Matthew 7: 15–17, 20
Revised Standard Version

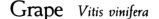

Grape *Vitis vinifera*

The grape, like the olive, had great symbolic significance in the Bible. It was so important that it was often referred to simply as "the vine." One of Noah's first acts after the flood waters had receded was to plant a vineyard, and a vineyard became a sign of prosperity and peace. The vine itself was a symbol of fruitfulness, regarded as a national emblem of the land of Israel.

The grape has been cultivated for so long that its origin is shrouded in mystery. By Biblical times in Palestine, the art of growing grapes and of making wine was almost as advanced as it is today. No soil and climate in the world is more suitable for the culture of grapes, and the Holy Land has always been famous for the luxuriance of its vines and the great size of its fruit clusters. The fruit was eaten fresh and dried as raisins, but it was primarily used for making wine—an important beverage in a land where water was scarce.

38

Grape

The Rod of Almond

When Moses and his brother Aaron led the people of Israel out of slavery in Egypt, their journey to the Promised Land of Canaan was filled with perils. The people were fearful and often wanted to turn back. "Were there no graves in Egypt that you have led us out here into the desert to die?" they asked. "Didn't we say, 'Leave us alone. We'd rather work for the Egyptians than die in the desert'?"

Time after time, God delivered them. He parted the waters of the Red Sea to let them walk through. He destroyed the Egyptian army that pursued them. He led the Israelites through the trackless land with a pillar of fire and cloud. God sent the people quail and manna to eat and caused water to gush forth from a rock, but still they complained.

A man named Korah decided to take advantage of the people's unhappiness and seize power from Moses and especially from Aaron, who had been appointed high priest. Why should Aaron be held in particular regard? "Aren't all God's people holy?" he demanded. "Isn't God with us each one? Why do you exalt yourself over the rest of us?"

Korah and his followers died because they rebelled, but the people still questioned Aaron's authority, so Moses told each family to bring a rod with the name of the head of the family carved on it. On the rod of the house of Levi, Moses carved Aaron's name. The rods were all presented in the great tent, or tabernacle, and the next day, when Moses went into the tabernacle, the rod of Aaron had sprouted. It budded and blossomed and bore ripe almonds. Thus God showed the children of Israel that Aaron and his household had been chosen as priests over all the people.

from Exodus and Numbers

Almond

Almond *Prunus dulcis*

The almond is the first tree to flower in the spring, and its lovely pink or white blossoms symbolize the awakening of the world after winter. The blossoms had a special religious significance for the Hebrews, who in ancient times carved them on the golden candlesticks in the tabernacle and who still carry them to the synagogue for festivals. Almonds were cultivated in the Holy Land centuries before Christ, and were mentioned in the Bible as one of the best fruit trees of the Land of Canaan. Introduced into the western world by the Phoenicians, they grew all around the Mediterranean and were an important article of commerce in central Europe during the Middle Ages.

The nuts are the kernels inside the seeds of small peachlike fruits. There are two varieties, sweet and bitter, both of which were known to the ancient Hebrews. Sweet almonds are valued for their edible nuts and for the pleasant oil derived from them, which can be used in soothing emulsions, in perfumes, and in cooking. Bitter almonds produce flavoring extracts and the poisonous glucoside amygdalin, once widely employed in medicine.

Jonah and the Castor-Bean Plant

When the Jews returned home after the exile in Babylon, their leaders demanded strict obedience to the ancient laws. In their desire for purity, however, the message of God's mercy for all nations was forgotten. Instead of preaching sermons about this truth, two people chose to tell stories. One told a love story, the story of Ruth, and the other—well, some people insist that the writer meant his account as solemn history. We think he intended otherwise.

Once long ago when Assyria was still a mighty power on the earth and Nineveh was the greatest of all cities, there lived in the tiny land of Israel a man whose name was Jonah.

One day God spoke to Jonah and said: "Arise, Jonah, and go to Nineveh, that great city in the east, and prophesy against it, for it is so wicked that I can hardly see the rest of the earth."

Jonah arose at once and went to the seaport at Joppa. But he boarded a ship bound for Tarshish, which was as far west as any boat set sail, for he was determined to escape the presence of the Lord and his impossible commands.

The Lord is not so easily left behind. He caused a great wind to blow and hurled it against the ship upon which Jonah sailed, so that the ship was about to break up in the storm, but Jonah was not afraid. He was curled up in the hold sound asleep.

The captain found him there and was very angry. "What do you mean sleeping?" he asked. "We are about to capsize! Wake up, you fool, and pray to your god. Maybe he will hear you and save us."

While everyone on the ship was praying furiously, no one's prayers prevailed against the storm. "Let us cast lots," the crew said, "and see on whose account this evil has come upon us." And they cast lots and the lot fell on Jonah. "Who are you?" they demanded. "What is your job, and where do you come from?"

Jonah answered, "My people are the Hebrews who worship the Lord God of Heaven, creator of both the sea and the dry land. I was a prophet of this God, but he told me to do something that no one could possibly do, so now I am running away from him. It is because of me that this storm has come up. Throw me into the water, and the sea will be quieted."

The sailors were unwilling to do such a terrible thing. They rowed as hard as they could, trying with all their might to bring the ship to shore, but the wind only blew stronger. So they prayed to Jonah's god and said: "Lord God, do not cause us all to die because of the sin of this man. And if, by chance, he is innocent, Lord God, do not hold his death against us." With that, they threw Jonah overboard, and immediately the sea was still.

But that was not the end of Jonah, for God had chosen an enormous fish that came along at that very moment and swallowed Jonah

Castor bean *Ricinus communis*

The plant that God appointed to grow and shade Jonah is, in some translations, called a "gourd plant" and sometimes simply a "plant." Growing, as the story relates, to a great height overnight, it is like the trees in the Garden of Eden—not a natural plant. But the best authorities think the writer means for his readers to imagine it as the castor bean, a nonwoody plant usually three to twelve feet in height, but sometimes much taller in the tropics. In hot climates it grows very fast and often seems like a tree, with huge umbrellalike leaves that make wonderful shade. The Hebrews valued the oil extracted from its beanlike seeds and used it widely in lamps and in ceremonial rites, but they do not seem to have used castor oil as the common medicine we know today.

46

Castor bean

whole. For three days and three nights Jonah sat in the belly of the fish until, at last, he prayed to the Lord to deliver him. So the Lord spoke to the fish, and it vomited Jonah up on the seashore.

Now the word of the Lord came to Jonah a second time. "Arise, Jonah, go to Nineveh, that great city, and proclaim to it the message that I will give you."

This time Jonah obeyed. He went to Nineveh and found a huge city—so large that it would take three days just to walk across it. Jonah went into the middle of the city and cried: "In forty days this city will be destroyed!"

When the people of Nineveh heard Jonah's warning, they believed the word of God and repented of their wickedness. They took off all their fine garments and put on sackcloth. Even the king of Nineveh got down from his throne, took off his royal robe, put on sackcloth, and went to sit among the ashes. "This is the word of the king," he said. "No one, neither man nor beast, is to eat or drink anything. Let everyone, man and beast, cover himself with ashes and cry unto God. Let him turn from his evil ways and the doing of violence. Perhaps, if we all repent, God will take back his anger and we will not perish."

And all the city of Nineveh from the least to the greatest repented of their wickedness. Everyone, even the cattle, wore sackcloth and sat among the ashes. God saw the penitence of Nineveh and was very pleased. All his anger was forgotten.

But Jonah was not pleased. He was furious. And he prayed to the Lord and said: "This is just what I thought. This is why I ran away to Tarshish in the first place. I knew you were a gracious God, slow to get angry, and of great mercy. I knew you would take back your judgment and fail to execute your anger. You have saved this wicked city and made a fool out of your prophet. Why don't you kill me? It would be better for me to die than to live." And Jonah pitched a tent on the east side of the city walls, and waited to see what God was going to do.

As Jonah sat there in the sun, he got very hot, so the Lord God caused a castor-bean plant to grow. It sprang up, and overnight, it had grown into a huge plant that shaded Jonah's head, for which Jonah was very glad. But the very next day God sent a worm to attack the plant, so that it withered. The sun beat down upon Jonah's head until he felt so faint he wanted to die. Jonah said again, "Just kill me. It is better for me to die than to live."

The Lord said, "Jonah, are you angry about the castor-bean plant?"

Jonah answered, "Yes, I'm angry. I'm so angry I could die."

And God said, "You are angry about that plant that you neither planted nor watered. If you feel sorry for a plant which came up in the night and withered in a night, can't you see why I feel pity for Nineveh? Why, there are a hundred and twenty thousand people there who can't even tell their left hand from their right, not to mention all those cattle."

after the Book of Jonah

49

Broad bean

NECESSITY

Some wandered in desert wastes,
finding no way to a city to dwell in;
hungry and thirsty, their soul fainted within them.
Then they cried to the Lord in their trouble,
and he delivered them from their distress;
he led them by a straight way,
till they reached a city to dwell in.
Let them thank the Lord for his steadfast love,
for his wonderful works to the sons of men!
For he satisfies him who is thirsty,
and the hungry he fills with good things.

from Psalm 107
Revised Standard Version

The Stew of Red Lentils

There has always been rivalry among sisters and brothers. Jacob was not above using food to trick his hungry brother into giving him what he wanted. In later years, Jacob made his peace with his brother Esau. At that time God changed his name from Jacob to Israel, and he became the father of the Israelite people.

When Rebekah, the wife of Isaac, gave birth to twin sons, the elder, who was red and hairy, was named Esau (which means "hairy") and the younger was named Jacob (or "heel holder"), for when they were born, Jacob was grasping his brother's heel. As the boys grew up, Esau became a hunter on the plains, but Jacob stayed close to the tents. Isaac loved Esau, but Rebekah loved Jacob.

One day when Esau came in from the fields, he was famished. His brother Jacob was cooking a stew of red lentils. The smell of the onions and lentils simmering in oil came to Esau's nostrils, and he said: "Give me some of that red stew before I starve."

But Jacob, who was born tugging at his brother's heel, remained a trickster. "All right," he said. "I'll give you some of this stew, but, first, sell me your birthright." Now the birthright belonged to the first-born son, and it meant that Esau would get a double share of their father's inheritance.

Esau said, "I'm dying of hunger. What use is a birthright to me?"

But Jacob held the pot out of reach. "First," he said, "you must swear."

So Esau swore, thus selling his birthright to his brother.

And Jacob gave him bread to eat as well as the stew, and Esau ate and drank and went on his way, forgetting the whole affair, so little did he cherish his birthright. But Jacob did not forget.

The day came when Isaac was old and blind and near to death, and he sent Esau out to shoot a deer, for he said, "I want you to prepare for me the savory food that I love, that I may eat it and bless you before I die."

Now Rebekah was eavesdropping at the door of the tent, and when Esau went out to hunt, she told Jacob what she had heard and commanded him to go to the flocks and choose two kids. "I will make them into the kind of savory dish that he loves. Then you will take it in to your father, so that he will eat it and bless you before he dies."

Jacob was frightened. "You know my brother is hairy and I am smooth," he said. "Suppose my father feels me and knows I am tricking him. He will curse me instead of blessing me."

But Rebekah was a clever woman. She put Esau's best clothes upon her son Jacob and covered his arms and his neck with goat skins and gave him the dish she had prepared. "Let your father's curse fall on me," she said.

So Jacob took the savory food in to his father. "Father," he said.

Isaac answered, "Yes, my son. Who are you?"

"I am Esau, your son," Jacob said. "I have prepared for you the savory food that you love. Come, sit up, and eat it, so that you may give me your blessing."

"How have you returned so quickly, my boy?"

"The Lord your God put success in my way," said Jacob.

But the old man was suspicious. "Come close to me. Let me touch you and know that you are truly my son Esau."

Jacob went close and let his father feel his arms. "The voice is the voice of Jacob," Isaac said, "but these are Esau's arms. Are you really my son Esau?"

"I am," said Jacob.

"Well, then," his father said, "give me some of the game, that I may eat it and give you your blessing."

Jacob served him food and wine and Isaac ate and drank. Then he said, "Come near, my son, and kiss me."

So Jacob came near and his father kissed him, and when he smelled Esau's clothes he said, "See, the smell of my son is as the smell of a field which the Lord has blessed. Therefore, may God give you the dew of heaven, and the fatness of the earth, and plenty of corn and wine. Let people serve you, and nations bow down to you. Be lord over your brothers, and let your mother's sons bow down to you. Cursed be every one that curses you and blessed be he that blesses you."

Isaac had hardly finished this blessing and Jacob had barely left his presence when Esau came in with the venison he had killed. He

Lentil

Lentil   *Lens culinaris*

The use of lentils is as old as civilization itself. They have always been a very important part of the diet of people in the Mediterranean region—and, indeed, throughout Europe. Their nutritious seeds are used in soups, and a kind of bread, very common in Egypt, is made of lentils and barley. In many countries, lentils are cut and threshed like grain.

Each small pealike pod contains only one or two seeds. Inside their brown or gray skins, the seeds may be yellow, red, orange, or green. The red variety that Jacob used for his stew was very frequently cultivated in Egypt and Palestine.

prepared a savory dish for his father and went into Isaac's tent. "Arise, father," he said, "and eat of this meat that you may give me your blessing."

Isaac began to tremble violently. "Who was just here?" he asked. "Who was it who brought me food so that I gave him the blessing which I cannot take away?"

When Esau heard this he cried out bitterly, "Oh, Father, bless me, too!"

But Isaac said, "Your cunning brother has come and stolen your blessing."

"He is rightly named Jacob," Esau said. "He has tricked me twice. First, he took away my birthright, and now he has taken away my blessing. But, oh, Father, haven't you saved a blessing for me?"

Isaac said sadly, "I made him your lord, and I have made all his brothers his servants. I have given him corn and wine. What is left for you, my son?"

"Do you have only one blessing, my father? Bless me too, Father," Esau cried out.

"Behold," said Isaac, "your dwelling shall be far from the fatness of the earth and far from the dew of heaven. You shall live by the sword and you shall serve your brother, but the time will come when you will break loose from his yoke."

Because of the stolen birthright, Esau's anger against his brother was very great, and he swore that after his father died and the days of mourning were past, he would kill Jacob. So Jacob fled the tents of his father and went to the land of Haran where his mother's people dwelt, and there he lived for many years.

from Genesis 27

Fruit of the Promised Land

When Moses brought the Israelites out of Egypt and across the Sinai desert to the edge of the Negeb, God directed him to choose twelve men, one from each of the twelve tribes, and to send them up through the Negeb to explore the hill country of Canaan, the land He had given to Abraham many years before.

So Moses sent twelve men to spy out the land. It was the season when the first grapes ripen. The men cut a bunch of grapes so large that they had to put it on poles and carry it between them. They also gathered pomegranates and figs. Canaan was indeed a rich land.

After forty days the men returned to the camp of the Israelites. The whole community gathered to hear their report. The men showed the people the fruit they had gathered in Canaan, and then they made their report to Moses. "We went up into the land as you told us to," they said. "Here is some of the fruit of the land. It is, as the Lord said, a rich land, flowing with milk and honey. But the cities are

Fig

Date

Pomegranate

Date *Phoenix dactylifera*

Fig *Ficus carica*

Pomegranate *Punica granatum*

Compared to the desert, Canaan must have seemed like a paradise, with its vineyards and its orchards of olives, figs, dates, and pomegranates. The fig still grows wild in Asia Minor, but it has also been cultivated since prehistoric times and, next to the grape, it was the Israelites' most valued crop, providing a large part of their daily food. The date palm grows wild from India to northern Africa, and it is the chief food plant of desert people. Both figs and dates were eaten either fresh or dried; fig fruits were used medicinally; and the sheaths of date clusters provided a sap that was used to make a kind of wine as well as a syrup called "honey" in the Bible. Though pomegranates were not a staple article of diet, they too have been cultivated since prehistoric times. The soft pulp around their seeds was either eaten raw or used in a spiced wine.

strongly fortified, and the people are giants—probably descendants of those demigods who lived on the earth in the time of Noah."

But Caleb interrupted. "We should go up immediately and occupy Canaan," he said. "I'm sure with the help of the Lord God we can conquer it." Joshua agreed, but the other ten discouraged the people. "We can't possibly conquer the land," they said. "If we go in there, we'll be swallowed whole. The people are giants, we tell you. Why, we'd look like grasshoppers to them."

When they heard this, the Israelites cried out in dismay, "If only we'd died in Egypt or even in the desert, how much happier we'd be! Why did God lead us here, only to have us die in battle and let our wives and children be carried off as trophies of war? It would be much better to go back to Egypt!" And they began to discuss among themselves who they would choose to lead them back.

Caleb and Joshua tore their clothes in frustration and shouted to the people. "The land we explored is a good land," they said. "It is flowing with milk and honey. God has given it to us. We don't have to fear the people of that land. God is on our side, not theirs. Don't rebel against him! Trust him. He will be with us."

In answer, the people picked up stones and were on the verge of stoning Joshua and Caleb, when, suddenly, the glory of the Lord appeared in the Tent of Presence. And God said to Moses: "How long am I going to have to put up with these complaining people? How much longer will they treat me with contempt and refuse to trust me? I am going to strike them down with a plague and deny them the heritage I promised them."

But Moses pled for the people, and God heard his prayer. The Lord did not immediately strike down the Israelites, but he said: "Out of all whom I brought out of Egypt and to whom I have shown my glory by many wonderful works, out of all those, only my servants Caleb and Joshua will be allowed to enter the land of promise. The rest will wander for forty years in this desert, and when this faithless generation has died, then I will let their children enter the land."

And so it was that out of all the thousands who left Egypt, only Joshua and Caleb lived to enter Canaan. Even Moses died before the conquest of the promised land, though God took him to the top of Mount Pisgah and let him look over and see the fruitful land spread out below.

from Numbers

A Harvest Love Story

After the Babylonian exile, Jewish leaders determined that the people should remain strictly separate from their heathen neighbors and declared that not only should there be no intermarriage, but those Jewish men who were already married to foreign women must divorce their wives. The writer of the Book of Ruth protested this policy with a love story in which the heroine was a foreigner.

Long ago, before the time of the kings, there lived in Bethlehem of Judah a man named Elimelech. Now it came to pass that a terrible famine arose in the land, and Elimelech took his wife Naomi and his two sons, Mahlon and Chilion, and went to live in the country of Moab. While they were there, Elimelech died. Naomi remained in Moab for about ten years, and her sons married Moabite women whose names were Orpah and Ruth. In time both Mahlon and Chilion died, leaving Naomi widowed and childless.

Since the famine in her homeland had ended, Naomi decided to leave Moab and return to Judah. Orpah and Ruth planned to accompany their mother-in-law, but Naomi said: "Go home to your mothers' houses, and may the Lord be as good to you as you have been to the dead and to me. And may the Lord give you each a new home with a new husband." And she kissed them.

Orpah and Ruth wept at the thought of leaving Naomi. "No," they said. "We will surely go to Judah with you."

But Naomi argued with them, "Think again, my daughters," she said. "I'm too old to have a husband. And even if I should lie and say I had any hope of marriage, or indeed if I should marry tonight and have sons, could you wait until they grew up to marry them? It breaks my heart for your sakes that I have no more sons to give you, but the hand of the Lord is against me."

With this the young women wept again. Orpah kissed her mother-in-law good-bye, but Ruth would not leave her. Naomi tried to persuade Ruth to go. "See," she said, "your sister-in-law has gone home to her people and to her gods. Go back with her."

But Ruth said, "Don't ask me to leave you or to return from following you. Wherever you go, I will go. Wherever you lodge, I will lodge. Your people shall be my people, and your God, my God. Where you die, I will die, and there I will be buried. May the Lord put his hand against me if anything other than death comes between you and me." When Naomi saw how determined she was, she said no more, and the two of them returned together to Bethlehem.

Naomi's old neighbors hardly recognized her. "Can this be Naomi?" they asked.

"No," she answered. "Don't call me Naomi any longer. Call me Mara, because the Lord has dealt bitterly with me." For the name Naomi means "Pleasant," while Mara means "Bitterness."

Since it was harvest time in Judah, and the two women had nothing to eat, Ruth decided to go to the barley fields to pick up the stalks which the reapers might drop; and it happened that the field that she went to glean belonged to a wealthy man named Boaz who was a kinsman of her father-in-law. Boaz saw Ruth and asked his foreman who the girl was.

"She's that Moabite girl that came back with Naomi," the servant answered. "She showed up early this morning and asked me to let her follow the reapers. She's been here ever since."

Then Boaz spoke to Ruth directly and told her not to glean in anyone else's fields except his. "Keep your eyes on the girls who reap for me and follow them wherever they go," he said. "I have told my men that they are not to bother you, and, if you get thirsty, ask one of my servants to give you water."

Ruth bowed herself humbly at Boaz's feet. "Why are you being so kind to me, a foreigner?"

Boaz answered, "I have heard all about you—all that you have done for your mother-in-law since your husband died—how you left your own father and mother and your native land and came to a land you did not know. May the Lord, under whose wings you have taken refuge, grant you a full reward."

Ruth marveled at these gracious words, for Boaz treated her as one of his own maidservants.

At the mealtime, Boaz sent for her. "Come and eat," he said, "and dip your bread into the wine." So Ruth sat among the reapers and Boaz himself passed her some parched grain.

When she got up to continue gleaning, Boaz instructed his reapers to let Ruth glean even among the sheaves. "Also," he said, "pull out some handfuls of barley from the bundles and leave them for her to pick up."

Ruth gleaned in the field until evening, and when she beat out the grain it came to about two thirds of a bushel of barley. She took it home to her mother-in-law.

Naomi was amazed. "Where did you glean today?" she asked.

"I was in the field of a man called Boaz," Ruth answered.

"God has not forgotten his goodness to the living and the dead," said Naomi. "This man Boaz is a near relative of ours, almost the next of kin. Stay close to his maidservants for Boaz will see that no one will bother you." So Ruth gleaned in the fields of Boaz until the end of the barley and wheat harvests.

Then Naomi said to her, "My daughter, I have determined to try to find a new home for you. Perhaps Boaz will do his duty as a kinsman and marry his cousin's widow. Tonight when the wind blows from the sea, he and his servants will be winnowing barley. I want you to bathe and anoint yourself and put on your finest clothes and go down to the threshing floor. Wait until they have all finished eating and drinking before you speak to him."

So Ruth did as she was told. After the work was over and the men had feasted, they lay down to sleep on the threshing floor so that no thieves would come to steal the heaps of winnowed grain. At midnight Ruth stole onto the floor to the place where Boaz was. The man was startled to find a woman on the threshing floor. "Who is it?" he asked, for it was too dark to tell.

"I am your servant, Ruth," she answered. "Please grant me your protection, for you are the next of kin."

"The Lord bless you, my daughter," he said. "This act is greater proof of your loyalty to your mother-in-law than the first. For you

Barley *Hordeum vulgare*
Corn poppy *Papaver rhoeas*

Grain is the oldest and most fundamental of man's food crops, and in Palestine barley rivaled wheat as a mainstay of existence. Being cheaper than wheat, it was the food of poor people and an important fodder for animals. It was most commonly used as a bread flour and as the malt in beer.

The story of Ruth points out how difficult life could be in Israel. Drought and famine came all too often to a land on the edge of the desert. But even when the famine was over, two widowed women had no way to obtain food, and without the opportunity to glean, they might have starved.

Until very recent times, planting and harvesting grain was done entirely by hand labor, and it required ceaseless toil through most of the year, from sowing time to reaping. The grain was usually cut with a sickle, and as each small bundle fell, it was gathered up, tied, and stacked. After the reapers had passed, poor people were allowed to glean the fields, picking up fallen heads of grain. Then the harvested crop had to be threshed. Beaten with a flail on a wooden floor, the grains were separated from their husks. Since they were heavy, they dropped to the floor, while the light bits of husk and straw were blown away by the wind.

The poppy is a common weed in the fields of Israel. It blooms when the grain is still green, before harvest time.

66

Barley

Poppy

haven't gone after any of the young men, rich or poor. Don't worry. I'll try to do what you ask. I am near kin, but there is one who is nearer. If he is willing to play the part of the next of kin, so be it, but if not, I swear that I will do it."

Boaz filled Ruth's cloak with barley to take back to her mother-in-law and sent her away while it was still dark, for Ruth was a virtuous woman, and he did not want it known that she had come to the threshing floor.

When she got home, Naomi was waiting. "How did it go, my daughter?" she asked.

Ruth told her all that Boaz had said and gave her the barley.

Naomi was pleased. "Just wait," she said, "the man will not rest until he has settled this matter."

Indeed, Boaz went to the gate of judgment that very day and waited until his kinsman came by. "Come, friend," he called to the man, and he had the kinsman sit down in the presence of ten elders of the city. "Our relative Naomi, who has returned from Moab, is selling a piece of land that belonged to our kinsman Elimelech. Now you are the next of kin, so if you wish to buy this land, do so now before this assembly of the elders, for you are the appropriate person to redeem Elimelech's land, but if you will not do it, I am next in line."

The kinsman answered, "I will redeem it."

Boaz continued. "Of course, when you buy the land, you are also obligated to marry Ruth, the Moabitess, the widow of Mahlon, Elimelech's son, so that you may provide your kinsman with heirs." For it was the law that if a man died without leaving children, his nearest kinsman was obliged to marry the widow, and the children of that marriage would be the heirs of the one who had died.

When the kinsman realized that he would be obliged to marry the Moabitess he said, "I cannot redeem this land for myself, because it will put my own inheritance in jeopardy. You may redeem it if you like." And, in accordance with the ancient custom, he took off his sandal and gave it to Boaz as a sign that he gave up all rights as next of kin.

Boaz called on the elders and the people standing nearby to witness to the fact that he would buy the land that had belonged to Elimelech and that he would marry Ruth the Moabitess, the widow of Mahlon, so that the name of the dead might not be cut off, but that his inheritance would continue in his native place.

Then all the elders and the people witnessed this transaction and asked the Lord to bless Ruth and give her many children and make the name of her house famous in Bethlehem.

So Boaz married Ruth and she bore a son, and Naomi took care of the child and called him Obed. And the women of Bethlehem said to Naomi: "Blessed be the Lord, for he has not left you without descendants, but he has given you this child to restore your life and nourish you in your old age, for your daughter-in-law who loves you, who has been better to you than seven sons, has borne this child."

And the child Obed, who was the son of Ruth the Moabitess and Boaz her husband, grew up and became the father of Jesse, who as everyone knows, was the father of David, the greatest king that Israel has ever known.

after the Book of Ruth

Myrtle

CELEBRATION

For you shall go out with joy and be led forth in peace.
The mountains and hills shall break forth before you
        into singing,
and all the trees of the field shall clap their hands.
Instead of the thorn shall come up the fir tree,
and instead of the brier, shall come up the myrtle tree;
and it shall be to the Lord for a name, for an everlasting
        sign that shall not be cut off.

after Isaiah 55:12—13

Flowers of Rejoicing

The wilderness and the dry land shall be glad,
    the desert shall rejoice and blossom;
like the crocus it shall blossom abundantly,
    and rejoice with joy and singing.
The glory of Lebanon shall be given to it,
    the majesty of Carmel and Sharon.
They shall see the glory of the Lord,
    the majesty of our God.

Isaiah 35: 1–2
Revised Standard Version

From a wedding song:

BRIDE

    I am like a wild flower in Sharon,
        a lily that grows in the mountain valley.

BRIDEGROOM

    Like a lily growing in the midst of brambles
    Is my beloved among women.

THE WOMEN

    Most beautiful of women,
        Where has your loved one gone that we may
        help you find him?

BRIDE

My beloved has gone to his garden,

there to his beds of spice,

to rejoice in the garden and to gather lilies;

I am my beloved's and he is mine,

he who takes delight in lilies.

after The Song of Songs 2:1–2; 6:1–3

I will heal their faithlessness;

I will love them out of the bounty of my love,

for my anger has turned from them.

I will be as dew to Israel;

he shall blossom as the lily,

he shall take deep root as the poplar;

his shoots shall spread out;

his beauty shall be like the olive,

and his fragrance like Lebanon.

They shall return and dwell beneath my shadow,

they shall flourish as a garden;

they shall blossom as the vine,

their fragrance shall be like the wine of Lebanon.

What has Israel any more to do with idols?

It is I who answer and look for you.

I am like an evergreen cypress which shelters you—

from me come all your blessings.

after Hosea 14:1–8

White lily *Lilium candidum*

Narcissus *Narcissus tazetta*

Iris *Iris pseudacoris*

Hyacinth *Hyacinthus orientalis*

Two species of lily grew in Palestine—the white Madonna lily and a very rare red one. The white lily, which is found in the mountains, is not especially rare, and it might well be the plant referred to in the Song of Songs. It might also be Isaiah's "crocus" (sometimes translated as "rose").

Lilies are referred to often in the Bible, but many of the references seem to describe some other flower. In fact, sometimes the word "lily" appears simply to mean "flower."

There are scholars who believe that at least some of the Bible's "lilies" are really wild hyacinths, which grow abundantly in fields and rocky places in the Holy Land, cloaking the land with a beautiful blue in springtime. The sweet-smelling polyanthus narcissus also grows very commonly in Palestine, and some authorities think it is Isaiah's "crocus," while Hosea's "lily" might be the yellow water iris that flourishes along the edge of streams in the same places poplars grow.

Since the true lilies grow only in the mountains, they could not possibly be Matthew's "lilies of the field," and nearly everyone believes these are anemones.

74

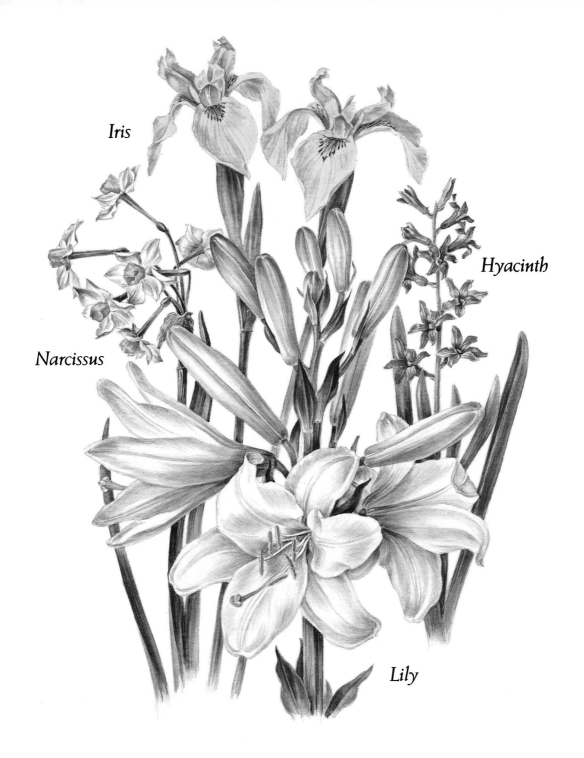

Iris

Narcissus

Hyacinth

Lily

Gifts of the Magi

He was called Jesus of Nazareth, the carpenter's son, yet the writer of the Gospel of Matthew tells that wise men from distant lands came to celebrate his birth, bringing gifts fit for a king.

Now when Jesus was born in Bethlehem of Judea in the days of Herod the king, behold, wise men from the East came to Jerusalem, saying, "Where is he who has been born king of the Jews? For we have seen his star in the East and have come to worship him."

When Herod the king heard this, he was troubled, and all Jerusalem with him; and assembling all the chief priests and scribes of the people, he inquired of them where the Christ was to be born. They told him, "In Bethlehem of Judea; for so it is written by the prophet:

'And you, O Bethlehem, in the land of Judah,
are by no means least among the rulers of Judah;
for from you shall come a ruler
who will govern my people Israel.' "

Then Herod summoned the wise men secretly and ascertained from them what time the star appeared; and he sent them to Bethlehem, saying, "Go and search diligently for the child, and when you have found him bring me word, that I too may come and worship him."

When they had heard the king they went their way; and lo, the star which they had seen in the East went before them, till it came to rest over the place where the child was. When they saw the star, they rejoiced exceedingly with great joy; and going into the house they saw the child with Mary his mother, and they fell down and worshiped him. Then, opening their treasures, they offered him gifts, gold and frankincense and myrrh. And being warned in a dream not to return to Herod, they departed to their own country by another way.

Matthew 2:1–12
Revised Standard Version

Frankincense *Boswellia carterii*
Myrrh *Commiphora abyssinica*
Rock rose *Cistus incanus*

Frankincense and myrrh are both fragrant resins produced by trees or shrubs that did not grow commonly in Palestine. They were imported from India, Arabia, or Africa and were therefore costly and precious.

Frankincense gum oozes from cuts in the bark of several species of Boswellia. Its yellowish or reddish drops become brittle and shiny as they dry, and when warmed or burned, they give off a strong fragrance, still used in church ceremonies. Myrrh from Commiphora, a thorny shrub or small tree, is an oily resin that oozes naturally from the stems, but can be increased by cuts in the bark. Bitter in taste, but very fragrant, it was used in medicine and was an important ingredient in holy oils and cosmetics. In Egypt, it was an embalming herb and a temple incense.

Another resinous gum sometimes called "myrrh" is ladanum, which comes from the rock rose, oozing during the heat of the day from the stems and leaves of this bushy little plant. It is still used in perfume and incense. The fragrant droplets are usually collected with rakelike instruments drawn gently over the plants, but in some places they are combed from the beards of goats that graze on the leaves. This is the myrrh of Genesis. In later times, it was used in medicine as well as perfume, and sometimes it replaced true myrrh or was mixed with it.

78

Myrrh

Frankincense

Rock rose

Anointing with Oil

There are many accounts of anointing in the Bible. The three that follow are examples of the different meanings of the custom, as a way of showing courtesy, respect, even devotion; for healing purposes; and as a symbol of the pouring out of God's Spirit.

Once Jesus was invited to dinner at the home of Simon, a Pharisee. The Pharisees were a leading religious party who believed in strict obedience to the laws of Moses. Now it was the custom in those days when a rich man gave a party, for people who had not been invited to come into the place where the party was being given and observe the festivities. There was in that town a woman who, when she heard that Jesus was eating at Simon's house, went there and sat down on the floor close to Jesus. She began to weep and her tears fell on his feet. She wiped his feet with her hair and kissed them. Then she anointed them with oil of myrrh which she had brought with her in a small flask.

When Simon, the host, saw what was happening, he was shocked and said to himself: "If this fellow were truly a prophet as they claim, he would know that this woman who is touching him is a notorious sinner."

And Jesus said: "Simon, I have something I want to say to you."

"Yes, master," Simon answered.

"Suppose," said Jesus, "that there were two men in debt to the same moneylender. One man owed him five hundred pieces of silver and the other man owed him fifty, but as neither could pay him anything at all, the moneylender forgave them both. Which of these two, do you think, would love him more?"

"Why, the one who owed him the most."

"You are right," said Jesus. Then he turned to the woman. "Do you see this woman?" he asked Simon. "When I came to your house today, you did not offer me water with which to wash my feet, but this woman has washed my feet with her tears and wiped them with her hair. You gave me no kiss of greeting, but this woman has hardly ceased to kiss my feet since she came in. You did not anoint my head with olive oil, but this woman has poured myrrh upon my feet. Her great love shows that her many sins have been forgiven. But the one who has few sins shows little love." Then he said to the woman, "Your sins are forgiven."

The other guests began to murmur among themselves. "Who does he think he is, that he can forgive sin?"

But Jesus said to the woman, "It is your faith that has made you whole. Go in peace."

after Luke 7: 36–50

One day when Jesus was speaking, a lawyer in the crowd decided to test Jesus, so he asked him: "Teacher, what must I do to receive eternal life?"

And Jesus, knowing that the man was well versed in the laws of Moses, said: "What is written in the law? What do you think the law says?"

The man answered, "Thou shalt love the Lord thy God with all thy heart and with all thy soul, and with all thy strength, and with all thy mind, and thy neighbor as thyself."

Jesus answered, "You've got the answer. If you do that, you will live."

But the lawyer was not satisfied. "Just who is my neighbor?" he asked.

Jesus answered this question, as he often did, by telling a story. "A man was traveling from Jerusalem down the lonely road to Jericho when he was attacked by robbers who stripped him of his clothes and all that he possessed, beat him and left him half dead by the side of the road. Now it happened that a priest was going down that road.

When he saw the man, who, for all the priest knew, was dead and therefore an unclean body, he crossed over to the other side of the road and passed on.

"In the same way, a Levite, who also had to keep himself pure for worship in the temple, came down the road, saw the man, and crossed over to the other side. But a Samaritan, who is thought to be an outcast by our people, as he came along the road, saw the man lying there and had compassion for him. He went to him, poured oil and wine upon the victim's wounds and bound them up. Then he set the man upon his own donkey and brought him to an inn and took care of him. The next day, when the Samaritan had to continue his journey, he gave the innkeeper money and said, 'Take care of this man, and whatever you spend, I will repay when I return.' "

And Jesus asked the lawyer, "Which of these three proved neighbor to the man who was robbed?"

The lawyer said, "The one who was merciful to him."

"Go," said Jesus, "And do as the Samaritan did."

after Luke 10:29—37

It came to pass that Saul was disobedient to the Lord, and the Lord was sorry that he had made him king of Israel. So the Lord said to Samuel his prophet, "How long will you mourn over Saul whom I have rejected? Take your horn of oil and go to the house of Jesse in Bethlehem, for I have chosen one of his sons to be the king of my people."

But Samuel said, "How can I anoint another king? Saul will hear about it and have me killed."

The Lord answered, "Take a young bull with you and say that you have come to sacrifice to the Lord and invite Jesse to come to the sacrifice."

As Samuel approached Bethlehem, the elders of the town heard of it and were afraid so they came out to meet him. "Why have you come?" they asked the prophet. "Do you come in peace?"

"Yes," said Samuel, "I come in peace to sacrifice to the Lord. Cleanse yourselves and join me in the sacrifice." Samuel himself invited Jesse and his sons to the sacrifice. When they came Samuel saw Eliab, the eldest son of Jesse, and he thought, "Surely this is the chosen king."

But the Lord said to Samuel, "Don't be fooled by his height or his good looks. I have not chosen him. The Lord does not see as people do. People judge by appearances, but the Lord looks into the heart."

One by one Jesse presented his sons to Samuel, until seven of his sons were brought to meet the prophet, but Samuel knew that none of them had been chosen by God. "Are these all your sons?" he asked Jesse.

Jesse answered, "I have one more, the youngest, but he is out taking care of the sheep."

"Send someone to bring him here," commanded Samuel, "for we cannot begin the sacrifice until he is here."

So they went and got David, a handsome boy with ruddy face and sparkling eyes. When he came in the Lord said to Samuel, "This is the one."

Samuel took the horn of oil and anointed the boy in the presence of his brothers, and the Spirit of the Lord came upon David and remained with him from that day on.

after I Samuel 16: 1–13

Olive

Eaglewood

Cassia

Olive *Olea europaea*

Cassia *Cinnamomum cassia*

Eaglewood *Aquillaria agallocha*

Important as it was for anointing, olive oil also had many other uses. People cooked with it, burned it in their lamps, and put it in soaps and cosmetics. In fact, the olive is among the most valuable of all plants in the region, and it is mentioned often in the Bible. Not only did it symbolize peace, revealing God's withdrawal of the flood, but its fruit and oil were used daily by all the people of the Middle East. In addition, its rich yellow wood is very hard and well suited for fine carpentry.

The branches of a wild olive are sparse and thorny, but the cultivated tree, with gnarled gray trunk and evergreen leaves, spreads a thick canopy. Growing very slowly, it lives to a great age, and some olive trees in present-day Israel are believed to be more than one thousand years old.

The holy oil used for anointing was usually scented with myrrh, aloes, cassia, or cinnamon. "Aloes," as used in the Old Testament, refers to the fragrant oil from the eaglewood tree, a precious commodity imported from Asia. (In the New Testament it is the same succulent plant we call aloe today). Cinnamon and cassia were also imported by the ancient Hebrews. They come from the bark of two closely related trees that are still grown for flavoring and medicine in Asia and the East Indies.

Palms Before the Lord

The righteous flourish like a palm tree,
they grow tall as a cedar on Lebanon;
    planted as they are in the house of the Lord,
    they flourish in the courts of our God,
vigorous in old age like trees full of sap,
    luxuriant, wide-spreading,
eager to declare that the Lord is just,
the Lord my creator, in whom there is no
    unrighteousness.

from Psalm 92:12–15
New English Bible

The Lord said to Moses: On the fifteenth day of the seventh month after the harvest has been gathered, you shall celebrate the Lord's Feast of Booths for seven days. The first day and the eighth day of the feast are days of rest. And on the first day you are to take citron fruit and palm branches and leaves of myrtle and willow branches from the riverside and you shall rejoice before the Lord. For seven days you shall live in booths, so that your children's children will be reminded that I caused their fathers and mothers to live in booths when I brought them up out of Egypt. For I am the Lord your God.

after Leviticus 23:33–44

The people who were with Jesus when he raised Lazarus from the dead went back to the city and reported the miracle to those who had come to celebrate the Feast of the Passover. When the crowd heard that Jesus himself was coming to Jerusalem, they took branches of palm trees and went out to meet him, crying:

"Hosanna! Blessed is he who comes in the name of the Lord!

God Bless the King of Israel!"

Jesus found a donkey and rode on it, just as the prophet Zechariah had written:

"Fear not, O daughter of Zion!

See! Your king comes, riding on a young donkey."

At the time his disciples did not understand what was happening; it was only after his resurrection they remembered the scripture.

But the Pharisees seeing the mob said to one another, "See? Nothing we do does any good. Look how the whole world goes after him."

after John 12:12–19

89

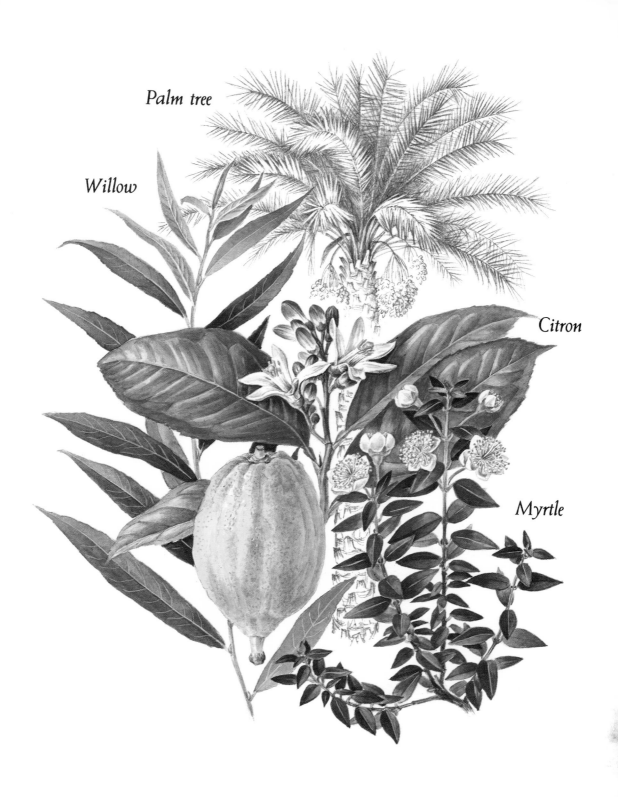

Palm tree

Willow

Citron

Myrtle

Palm *Phoenix dactylifera*
Citron *Citrus medica*
Willow *Salix alba*
Myrtle *Myrtus communis*

The people of the Holy Land saw the date palm as a sign of majesty and fruitfulness, rising as it did to heights of more than eighty feet. The huge leaves were symbols of triumph, often carried in ceremonies, but they were also used for roofing, fencing, and the making of mats, baskets, and dishes. Rope was made from the fibrous material in the crown of the trees. The trunk was used for timber, and the date fruit was food for animals as well as people. It is said that the date palm has more uses than the year has days.

The palm was, along with the citron, myrtle, and willow, one of the "four species" that still play an important part in the Jewish Festival of the Booths, or Succoth. The citron, or ethrog, is a lemonlike fruit, which symbolizes fertility and abundance. Jewish tradition has long believed it to be the "goodly tree" listed in the original Hebrew words of this passage from Leviticus. Myrtle, a low bush or small tree, was very common in the Holy Land. Its sweet-smelling leaves and flowers were regarded as a symbol of immortality and peace and divine generosity, and they were also the source of fragrant oil and sachet powder. There is much disagreement about the various "willows" of the Bible, and in some cases, the word seems to refer to the Euphrates poplar. But the willow of the four species was a true willow and it symbolized the water needed for good harvests.

The Tree of Life

And I saw a new heaven and a new earth: for the first heaven and the first earth were passed away; and there was no more sea. And I John saw the holy city, new Jerusalem, coming down from God out of heaven, prepared as a bride adorned for her husband. And I heard a great voice out of heaven saying, Behold, the tabernacle of God is with men, and he will dwell with them, and they shall be his people, and God himself shall be with them, and be their God. And God shall wipe away all tears from their eyes; and there shall be no more death, neither sorrow, nor crying, neither shall there be any more pain: for the former things are passed away. . . .

And the angel showed me a pure river of water of life, clear as crystal, proceeding out of the throne of God and of the Lamb. In the midst of the street of the city, and on either side of the river, was there the tree of life, which bare twelve manner of fruits, and yielded her fruit every month: and the leaves of the tree were for the healing of the nations.

Revelation 21:1–4, 22:1–2
King James Version

Scriptural References

NEW TESTAMENT

Index of Plants

Page numbers in **bold** indicate illustrations

96